In the Truth Room

Other Volumes in the Series

The Morse Poetry Prize

Edited by Guy Rotella

DANA ROESER

In the Truth Room

THE 2008 MORSE POETRY PRIZE

Selected & introduced by Rodney Jones

NORTHEASTERN UNIVERSITY PRESS
  Boston
PUBLISHED BY
  UNIVERSITY PRESS OF NEW ENGLAND
  Hanover & London

Northeastern University Press
Published by University Press of New England
One Court Street, Lebanon, NH 03766
www.upne.com
© 2008 by Dana Roeser
Printed in the United States of America
5 4 3 2 1

Library of Congress Cataloging-in-Publication Data
Roeser, Dana, 1953–
In the truth room/Dana Roeser; selected & introduced
by Rodney Jones.
    p. cm. — (The 2008 Morse Poetry Prize)
ISBN 978-1-55553-697-8 (pbk.: alk. paper)
I. Title.
PS3618.O38152   2008   811'.6 — dc22   2008033379

University Press of New England is a member of the
Green Press Initiative. The paper used in this book meets
their minimum requirement for recycled paper.

For Don, Eleanor, & Lucy

Contents

Acknowledgments

Thanks to the editors of the following journals, in which these poems, sometimes in different versions, first appeared: *Antioch Review:* "In the Truth Room," "What Did the Children Know and When Did They Know It?"; *Barrow Street:* "The Flossie Stories"; *Controlled Burn:* "On Mount Saint Francis: Over Goldengrove Unleaving"; *Ellipsis:* "My Father Gave Us a Wendy-Bird"; *Harvard Review:* "Swerve"; *Northwest Review:* "If You Step Off Now," "He Read the New Yorker Aloud to Me and Spoonfed Me Pieces of Cantaloupe: Le Coup de Foudre," "Summer Meditation for Paul: Ajuga, Look Back," "Terminal"; *Notre Dame Review:* "The Fire of London"; *Paterson Literary Review:* "Leaving the House on Bobolink"; *Prairie Schooner:* "Maple Tree: Wound"; *Shade:* "Night"; *Shenandoah:* "Mud Cap"; *Southern Review:* "Invisible Men," "Psychoanalytic Vacation"; and *Sou'wester:* "Autumn Is Cusp" and "Midwestern Summer: My Dead Mother as Muse."

"Midwestern Summer: My Dead Mother as Muse," "What Did the Children Know and When Did They Know It?," and "Mud Cap" appeared on *Poetry Daily.* "If You Step Off Now" appeared on *Verse Daily.*

For their generous help with these poems, both individually and in manuscript form, I would like to thank Hilene Flanzbaum, Mary Leader, David Dodd Lee, Daniel Morris, and Donald Platt. For his sensitive, insightful editing of this manuscript, special thanks to Guy Rotella, Series Editor, and for choosing this book and writing the introduction, my thanks to Rodney Jones.

A fellowship from the National Endowment for the Arts aided significantly in the completion of this book. I would also like to acknowledge the support of the Jenny McKean Moore Writer-in-Washington

Fellowship at George Washington University, Butler University, and the following artists' colonies: Yaddo, the Virginia Center for the Creative Arts, Le Moulin à Nef (VCCA France), Ragdale Foundation, and Mary Anderson Center for the Arts.

Introduction

There is an artificial element in the process of reading manuscripts for a poetry book competition. To begin with, one reads from the beginning, not randomly or backward. Also, one cannot dodge the sense that one is judging, not just reading, and frequently, after numerous readings, when a decision is made, it is difficult to shake the notion that, on another day, perhaps if one had eaten oatmeal instead of blueberry scones for breakfast, another book would have been chosen. On rare occasions, however, by dint of talent and passion, a book will issue a mandate. Dana Roeser's second collection, *In the Truth Room*, was such a book for me. From my first encounter with the opening line, "I love the night," I found myself in the grip of a boldness and clarity that distinctly resembled mastery, and it was not simply the artistry I was responding to, but the book's powerful and complex vitality.

Unlike prose, poetry is seldom categorized or taught as fiction or nonfiction, though clearly, after the Second World War, much of the best American poetry could be seen as creative nonfiction, of both the objective essay type and the memoir. It seems important to note that, while Roeser brings considerable lyrical dexterity to a variety of individual poems, the aggregate of *In the Truth Room* suggests the shape and necessity of a life, at once dramatically compelling and immediately believable, one in which children are eating s'mores while watching a *Fawlty Towers* video, and Volvos are skidding on ice, and people are going to 12-step meetings, museums are being visited, and jobs and essential human relationships hang in the balance.

On the face of it, the story at the center of the book seems archetypal: a daughter in midlife making sense of ongoing experience in the wake of her mother's death while dealing with substantial crises and, eventually, undertaking what amounts to a pilgrimage. The overarching theme is individual, feminist, contemporary: How does a woman know herself apart from convention and duty? Certainly the intense poems about the mother are a key to this theme. But *In the Truth Room* is less about one life than a fabric of interwoven lives: four generations of family, friends, dear ones, present and departed—I would be hard-pressed to name a poetry book that develops and displays affection for more characters or, for that matter, one that contains more life.

Roeser gives us a number of poems that do not pertain directly to the main flow of the book, poems like "Invisible Men," an account of a night visit to a 24-hour Kinko's that suggests something of the magic of Wallace Stevens's "Disillusionment of Ten O'Clock," or "Summer Meditation for Paul: Ajuga, Look Back," a prayer for a young friend with melanoma, but even in these poems, she works with quick, bold strokes, an acute sense of metaphor, and an imaginative clarity that she perhaps best articulates at the end of "The Fire of London," when she says of Edward Hopper (and perhaps her own project): "Hopper's goal, to follow Goethe, to / reproduce the 'world that / surrounds me by means of the / world that is in me'—the philosophy, the / flame of it."

The staggered, heavily enjambed lines that Roeser favors are themselves part and parcel of her restless energy, which perhaps shows itself best in the longer pieces—"Maple Tree: Wound," "He Read the New Yorker Aloud to Me and Spoonfed Me Pieces of Cantaloupe: Le Coup de Foudre," "Autumn Is Cusp," and "Swerve," a frightening poem of a near-death experience, which is surely the turning point in the subliminal narrative of this book. I love these longer poems because they are all over the place, fearless, unmistakably true. And while they make leaps in register and subject, these leaps never seem merely theatrical or aesthetic by design, but the natural propensity of a large mind that is open at every instant to realizations that less capable poets might narrow to tragic or comic effects.

I did not know when I selected *In the Truth Room* as the Morse winner that Ellen Bryant Voigt had chosen *Beautiful Motion*, Roeser's previous book, as the 2004 winner, but it does not surprise me. Roeser's poetry squares with many of our favorite maxims, with Yeats's statement that rhetoric is what we make out of our quarrels with others while poetry is what we make out of our quarrels with ourselves, or with Stevens's insistence that poetry should be a clear statement of mixed emotions. Roeser has the courage to be many things at once: domestic and wild, experimental and articulate. I would like to put *In the Truth Room* in many parts of the bookstore: grief and healing; humor; feminism; religion; memoir—but only because the books in these sections sell more than poetry. There is a special quality of attention in the best poetry that is like light, and it has very little to do with strategy. It comes from authentic emotion and it aspires to art. Roeser brings that quality to every page.

Rodney Jones

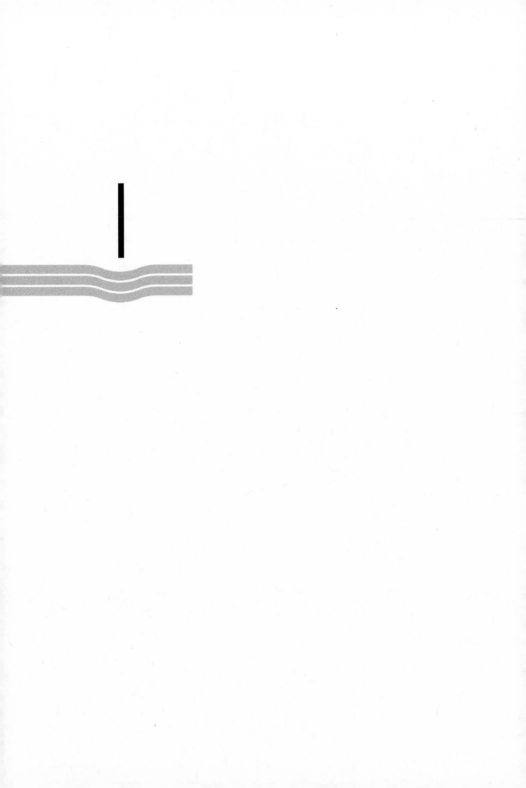

Night

I love the night. In the morning,
my husband's mother loves him and bakes him
an apple pie. In the morning, he

wakes early and writes clever
poems to place on her doorstep. My time is the night.
Negative of his positive. The world

in which I am loved — because it is
not the world. But the world's moon, its reflection. My mother
only wanted to nap. I can see that

now, because I have become her.
It was not the nap. At three in the afternoon.
It was the solitude. It was

reprieve from daylight. She made a stab
at the tourist hot spots, the wholesome outings. By
afternoon she couldn't stand the homilies,

the group leg iron. She had to go
to bed! I am just like her. My father's new girlfriend
hands me the tourist highlights

from the local paper—the boardwalk
art show and dolphin jumping—
and I hand it directly

to my husband. My father's new
girlfriend is a morning person. She doesn't have a
mean streak. After one hundred years of

terror, we flock to her,
cling to her daylight. She says the words
my mother said, calls my father

by his nickname, but it's weirdly substanceless,
like suddenly she's the night and my mother,
day. My mother had

dark hair and Ellen has light,
and so on. My mother had the courage of her convictions.
She did not do yoga. She did

not get massage. She liked a
rare steak and a glass of whiskey—but only one. All things
in moderation, even her lurid dying. She

said, We Ladies of the Old
South rise above it; she carried *The Way of All Flesh* in
her blue night bag for her last

trip to the hospital. She knew she was
out of air. She knew that nowhere on earth, in this life,
was there enough oxygen for her.

I wept for six months
about her life. About how there was no
        element for her. She never

        looked comfortable,
not in her childhood photos and portraits,
        not in all the years I knew her. She

        came to life a little in
the twilight. Her once-daily cigarette at sunset
        on the beach. She loved the shore,

        the margin, the entrance to
the wild, other, world. I wept because living
        seemed agony to her, and love,

        the worst. I kept saving things
to tell her. Most of the letters I wrote to her, I tore up
        or put aside. I was saving stories

        for that other place, our own
dead letter office, a place without shadow,
        that paradise, the night.

Invisible Men

Kinko's is open 24 hours
and I love to go at night
        when the air is thin

        and most of this resort
is asleep. The roads
        like silk. Police

        camped out at all
the major intersections
        dozing. Me in my

        car with the windows rolled
up belting it out with
        Aretha Franklin, a danger

        to no one. At Kinko's
I see a man sitting before a computer
        as though at work—

        a perfect imitation
of a working man, his notebooks
        open, supersized soft drink cup

with straw inserted
next to him. Yet I realize finally
      he is entirely

        asleep. Later, on my
way to the bathroom, I see
      another man —

        a dark man with a white
woolly cap of hair — at another
      terminal, in the same

        pose. So still he could be
covered with snow. A real go-getter.
      Like Segal's dead-white

        figures facing forward
on the subway. The Kinko's workers must
      assiduously avoid asking

        themselves why these two
men — others — haven't moved for hours. Their
      willingness to sleep this

        way is too touching, too
enterprising. A Kung Fu
      trick, a Batman trick, to make

        oneself invisible. Fighting off
my own rigor, I jab the keyboard,
      peppering my e-correspondents

with passionate exhortations.
Then I remove my long-suffering
          credit card, make my way to

          the car and the
slumbering beach house. I leave
          my friends the statue-men

          to soldier on,
propped at their work stations, in
          poses of critical

          deliberation. May they
awake restored, knowing they are the
          linchpins of some alternate

          night economy, under
the fluorescent lights of Hilltop Shopping Center's
          24-hour Kinko's.

What Did the Children Know and When Did They Know It?

What Did the Animals Know and
When Did They Know It?
    Wall Street Journal, Jan. 4, 2005

I kept the secret well.
A tsunami had struck Southeast Asia
    and 43,000 people were killed. That's

        what they said at first, somewhat
loudly, somewhat pointedly, somewhat unmistakably,
    on the radio, on the day after Christmas.

        But the girls were playing
Yahtzee, or watching that hilarious *Fawlty Towers*
    video for the nth time, or

        practicing their dance steps, or doing
each other's hair, or toasting s'mores through the
    side door of the woodstove,

        the Christmas tree winking
at us from the other room, not yet as dry
    as tinder, and though

9

I didn't turn the radio off — and
it kept going on and on, the steady accretion of
horrific detail — it somehow

couldn't compete with their
industrious pursuit of the funny video, or the
violin, their absorption

in the s'mores, or whatever
it was that they were doing. I didn't
turn it off; I let it talk

alongside them, wondering
when they would notice, sort of incredulous
that they hadn't, but not wanting

to stop them, to say something.
Now, reading the Wall Street Journal
today, a week later,

I realize that they, like the antelope
stampeding the shoreline in the state
of Tamil Nadu — ten minutes

before the tsunami hit — or the elephants,
leopards, deer, and other wild animals
who escaped unharmed in Sri Lanka,

had already found high land,
a little island, that
would not break. You see,

I wasn't just keeping
the secret of the tsunami. There was something
else in the house. How often

I'd wished they'd overhear,
preferably my side of the story, so that I would not
have to know alone. But my girls had

already proceeded inland.
They were balancing on their new exercise
balls from Borders, watching John

Cleese, as Basil Fawlty — with the
woman in the video, "Polly," the maid, who in real
life was, for a long while, at least,

his wife — his helpless antics
in the face of events that he couldn't control,
events that became all the more

idiotic and perverse, as he
tried to twist them in service of his petty pride
and vanity, and we all died

with laughter watching him,
balancing on our balls, holding our secrets
in our mouths like big marbles.

Leaving the House on Bobolink

Perennials don't really know anything, I've noticed.
    They pop their scrawny heads up no matter what, grow lush.

And my father's lettuce bolts, towers, spindles, turns to dust.
    I was there the day my mother left the house for good,

house of hummingbird and basil, gardenia and foxglove.
    I don't know if she was looking out of the window

or not, even knew what was going on. She was so ill
    she was blue, her fingernails, the bottom half of her face.

I saw no reason to rush her to the doctor.
    I gave her a tissue for her nose. She removed

the oxygen tube to wipe it. She had to rest
    for several minutes before she could stand. I carried

her black-and-white-patterned cloth purse
    and my father carried her oxygen. For some reason,

he kept pushing her, or pulling her, to be more accurate,
    and I kept telling her to slow down. As

they walked through the rooms and to the car. Mother
        said, I don't want to scare the children. Don got

in the other car with the girls. I got in the back seat.
        My mother in the front seat

gasping. My father driving a bit lurchingly
        so that the unsecured oxygen tanks in the back

rolled against each other, the dolly, and the big portable
        machine that converted ordinary air to oxygen

for home use. Finally, there wasn't enough oxygen
        anywhere and she went into the hospital,

was put under some kind of high-powered mask.
        The voices on the phone came as from

under water: *Don't come. You better get up here.*
        She's not doing well. She wants to be alone. She

wrote a note. She wants her wallet taken
        back to the apartment. She'd been halfway into her second

night at the apartment when she gave up and
        went with my dad to the emergency room.

I left her that day, in daylight, with
        my daughters. She was leaning forward on her bed,

wearing sweats and a fleece vest. She told my younger
        daughter to look at the pelicans fly by

the eleventh floor window, the wind surfer
      under the giant multi-colored kite, seagulls.

There's no telling what you might see,
      she said. She loved her new room. The apartment

three years in the building and planning. She never got
      to the living room to see the sofa in the place

she'd chosen for it, or the bookshelves. She told
      me to look out for the Queen's Bird china when I was

unpacking. To put it under the dry sink.
      She was going to give it to Lucy. And Eleanor

Beckham's silver to my Eleanor. We had a nice talk and
      leaned, each of us, to kiss her goodbye. The girls

were sweet. *Love you, love you, love you.* We left then.
      Coming out of the bathroom

I saw her but did not call to her, not wanting
      to strain her again. She was sitting, still

leaning forward in that unnatural
      position. Still breathing hard. Looking at her hands.

Studying her hands—raised rivers and tributaries
      of vein. Thinking, perhaps, of the next

minute, and the next.

The Fire of London

Thomas Farrinor (or Faynor), a baker in Pudding Lane, just
north of Billingsgate fish market, failed to put out the fire
under his oven. His house caught light. Flying sparks fired the
Star Inn on Fish Street Hill. A Thames Street tallow-chandler's
went up in flames, which were fanned by a strong east wind.
Roy Porter, *London: A Social History*

In this bottom bunk, under
the white wire mesh of my
husband's bottom,

I try not to panic. Stalactite
plastic wallpaper, a dirty cream-color, to
my left. *Those rats in the*

underground, under the tracks.
It is summer and I can't
decide if my favorite

is the man playing the
kazoo on the first leg of the straightaway
that leads to the Northern

or the one in sunglasses
in a crook in the tunnel
at Tottenham Court Road.

He plays jazz on his
electric guitar, has his drum
machine set at

a good snare
pace. The effect is liquid
late Santana. He doesn't

look angry, bitter, in those
mirrored sunglasses, or even
unhealthy, at the end of the

people-sized cylinder
where it turns left
and shoots us down a quick flight

of stairs to the platform —
the track headed west to
Notting Hill Gate. Right before the turn

for the stairs, facing you, is
a large black and white poster, advertising
meditation — how?

At St. Martin-in-the-Fields,
the chamber orchestra plays
Haydn, Mozart's Clarinet

Concerto, Requiem. It is
so sonorous/gorgeous, it doesn't seem
        like music. Certainly, no relation

        to my hacking attempts
at reading notes, keeping time on the
        piano. St. Martin-in-the-Fields,

        three-hundred-year-old
bottle of wine, acoustics so perfect they
        cannot be replicated, so

        all of the recordings are done
here, a strip of numbered tape along the backs
        of pews to assign seating.

        It only happens, can happen,
here, that sound — and the orchestra
        members, the chorus, down

        in the "Café in the Crypt" in the
interval, sipping wine and eating
        salmon pie, casual as you

        please. St. Martin-in-the-Fields
is under renovation, but you
        can bet they won't touch

        the sanctuary, sacred decanter.
This hotel room weirdly
        smells like fire and I

remind myself it is simply
the sloughed skin of many hostel
    dwellers before us, their stench.

        Directions posted on the wall:
"Attack the fire with the appliances
    provided," and if that doesn't work,

        "Find the 'way out.'" No,
of course it's not the fire of London,
    the cloven tongues

        of fire over the woman's, Shelly's,
and the man's — Duncan's —
    heads, at the 12-step meeting

        in Chelsea — those little
Pentecostal hell flames. She
    attempted suicide two days

        ago — yes, she knew it wasn't
advised to get involved
    with someone in the program. And Duncan

        said he got so bollixed up
trying to figure out whether
    or not to say an official goodbye

        to his children and what
method to use (and whether he'd
    have to drink again to pull it off),

he duly reported his confusion
to his rehab counselor, who calmly
        referred him to a printed list of "relapse

        triggers," in which his behavior
could be found. Edward Hopper
        was fascinated with light,

        was convinced the light
on the second story of a building at sundown
        was different, more ecstatic, than

        on the first. At a retrospective,
at the Tate Modern, I see each Hopper person—
        the woman at the diner counter

        in "Nighthawks," picking
at something (a piece of paper, a tea bag?),
        the pensive man staring out a

        window, smoking, in "Hotel
by a Railroad"— struggling
        in her/his own personal

        hell flame, grappling with her/his
hamartia, the death they are
        destined for: death by

        disappointment, resignation,
prostitution, compromise, death by
        suffocation. Achilles' and Hector's

heroic deaths at the British Museum,
with Athena behind
and Apollo turning away, respectively,

as preordained. Or the other vase, on
which the warriors fight
nude, exposed as Hopper's

"Woman in the Sun." The miniature
cat-sized sarcophagus in the British Museum
with sculpted cat head, startled

cat face, above. The sand-blasted
2000-plus-year-old human corpse in a
fetal curl, repositioned

as in a tomb with its
important, sacred, everyday objects around it—
vases, drinking cups, grooming tools,

beads, coins. Even the horrifying
masks suspended from the ceiling in the "Living and
Dying" exhibit, meant to keep

away the horrid devil—still and
kinesthetic at once—contain the breath and
power of the Holy Spirit.

The statue of Albert, Prince
Consort, dipped in gold, slumps above Bayswater,
the known world at its base.

Tableaux representing "architecture,"
"commerce," "engineering," "agriculture." At each
corner, three-dimensional Asians

on an elephant, Africans on a
camel, Americans on a buffalo, Europeans
on an ox. And above

him: Victoria, of course, Greek
gods and goddesses, Jesus, Mary, their God,
and numerous seraphim. The dull-

eyed guard at the hostel, from Ghana,
all day standing by the cement steps.
Immigrant men in their

immobilizing sandwich boards
on Queensway, one hawking McDonald's
chicken sandwiches, the other, computers.

This fetid room: it hurts
to breathe the air. At St. Martin-in-the-Fields,
candles lit all over the sanctuary —

the fire of London started
this way, a wick and a flame. (How glad I was
to hear them speak, at the

meeting, of suicide. Shelly.
Duncan.) In one Hopper painting, "Excursion into
Philosophy," originally called

"Excursion into Reality," a man,
clothed, sitting bedside, staring down at a panel
of sunlight on the carpet, a book

(Plato, his wife says in the
catalogue notes) downturned beside him, woman
behind with her back

to him, her skirt hiked up,
her naked bottom — like my husband's
pajamaed rear-end close to my

face in the reeking London House
Hotel room. Hopper's goal, to follow Goethe, to
reproduce "the world that

surrounds me by means of the
world that is in me'" — the philosophy, the
flame of it.

Summer Meditation for Paul
Ajuga, Look Back

The world is an
aggressive place. World on the march.
In the garden, purple ajuga puts out

its feelers, runners, roots;
colonizes, won't look back. What is
breath? In a light-bombarded

room: Noise. Roofers pound.
Tree clippers buzz. Snowplow scrapes
the street, preps for

paving. Opaque, sightless
trucks beep, back, push. *Look out!* Let nature
take its course: Let the sperm

win the derby, make Alicia
pregnant. But not the melanoma. Men in dark
suits jostle, shoulder, elbow,

will not yield space. They will
go to the wall. Military persons. *Save
Paul.* He is 24, 6 3½. He grew

yesterday. Every cell shimmers,
but not the malignancy. Dark splotches
under a chestnut tree on a

cloudless July day.
Not motiveless. *Save
Paul.* Look back, ajuga.

Maple Tree
Wound

The extended metaphor: "the
emblem of yourself, if you like, or of
someone, or something, else." Coming

home from lunch
with Tom and Mary, where I got a little
relief, a little temporary

relief, from the agony
of always hustling for the next thing, I take
a stick to the bolus

of solidified pus — on the knot,
on the bare place — is it the amputation
place? — of a limb —

of the giant maple
that dominates my life. Once
I touched the white lump with my

fingers. Lucy was with me.
It had a kind of wetness, a kind of sweat. Disgusting.
Ruth will not let up with

the cognitive therapy shit.
I know exactly what she's up to. I've read about
it. Just keep telling the "client"

that he/she is fine. That will
change the pattern of the negative thinking about
him/herself. What kind of fool

does she take me for? Perched
on her chair like that? I couldn't believe
how sweaty and revolting

that glob. I washed my hands
a thousand times after touching it. Rapacious
maple. Its wound doesn't seem to be

slowing it down any. Our "perennial
garden," put in by Shelly, gardening consultant,
is half the size, height, and

heft of Danny and Felicia's
next door. Whose garden gets full sun
and no root interference. Who do

not have the greedy maple. I saw
a maple tree, in the Bonsai Club display, at
Global Fest. Grown from one of those

wingy things, whirligigs.
They gave the date it was started as
twelve years ago. It was about a

five-inch-long twig, but with its
junior canopy of leaves. It was planted
in something china, a little holder of

some kind, looked a bit pinched.
It was in with the poodle-like shaped bonsais—
must have been a bit

chagrined. Metaphor!
Where art thou? Really. Am I the maple or the
gaping wound or the surprisingly

firm, obdurate mass of whitish
excrescence poufing from the wound. Does it grow?
Has it grown in the four

years that we've been here? Is it,
at certain times of the year, more liquefied/
putrefied? I think of the horrid

discussions about trans-fatty acids.
Oops, I mean trans-fats. Is that what
I mean? Anyhow, it's the kind

of oil that becomes solid at
room temperature, also known as
hydrogenated fat. I've

already got some
of the waxy stuff within, hence the
agonizing abstinence from fried

calamari (how can "fried"
be a problem linked with "calamari"?). I'm
        sorry the tree is bleeding.

                Is suppurating. I'm sorry, dear
tree, which in truth I have not found
        dear. Half its leaves bedraggle, come

                in late or not at all, die
brown before the first frost. The tree
        does not look altogether healthy.

                Ruth! I said, Oh, for
God's sake, Ruth, let's face
        it, I'm handicapped. She nodded

                but then went right on with
her positive-thinking agenda. God! Who gives
        a shit about my wound? I can

                hardly remember what it is. Or the
glob of suet that hangs off of it. Or the leaves
        not coming all the way in, or the young

                maple cosseted by some misguided
Bonsai aficionados in a china pot? There's something
        to be grateful for—I was not

                raised in a china pot. (My wound,
I think, was less awful than my mother's. And
        more awful, I pray, than my daughter's.) Wait.

Whoa. Where went the
metaphor? And, promise me, you'll never let my students
        see this. Not that they care one

                way or the other. They do not.
Not caring. Was that the wound? No. I have
        neglected the tree. As I do all living

                things in my life requiring
my care. Benign neglect, an expression I learned
        somewhere. Right. I have tried

                to love my daughters (love as
in action verb, as in St. Francis). It is true
        that I refused to take Eleanor to her

                allergy shot during her
English class, for which she was unprepared. That
        was a good thing.

                True also, that after I pick
up Lucy, I'll want nothing more than to lie
        face down on the bed. She'll be

                okay with that. She has homework
or some hoops to shoot / goofing around to do. The
        metaphor! Ruth! Cognitive

                therapy. Vs. Jungian. Ruth got
alert on that one, said I couldn't just waltz in and
        start to see Paul's therapist without

asking his permission (she remembered
the lengths I went to to keep Jane from seeing *her!*). I don't
want to say I'm wounded and always

will be. It sounds so lame! The maple
tree is lovely, or lovely enough. Has copious babies,
the whirligigs, some of which try to

become real fledgling trees in our
gutter. The tree whispers outside my upstairs bedroom
window, winter and summer, and drapes

its lower leaves into my study
window below. The tree has been trying to
be my friend this whole time. I must forgive

it its greed. Its heavy-feeding
roots. It is a needy maple. It has to feed that glob
of "I Can't Believe It's Not Butter" or

"Smart Balance Lite," or suet,
or Crisco, or Blue-Bonnet-On-It, or the whipped unsalted
real butter that Eleanor Beckham, my step-grandmother,

served at her brownstone in New York City
in the '60s. It was years before I really got to
know her. She shed an entirely different,

and seemingly clearer, light on my
family. *Evil stepmother. Carbuncle. Narcissist.*
Oh, she wasn't any of those. She had

a pearl-handled revolver and left
my philandering grandfather with only a
        $1000 check in hand. That hunk

        of suet, of ooze, should
not be seen. Is meant to be invisible. We all have
        something. Ruth, denial queen,

                has something, but I'm only privileged
to sense it, not know it. It is time to pick Lucy up!
        Shine on, big maple!

                Shine on, Eleanor Beckham! May
the living and the dead and their visible / invisible
        excrescences continue

                to walk with me. As trees walk, as Tom
and Mary, other beloved friends— living and dead—
        walk, more important

                than some balloon of wrongedness,
or sorrow, that I can't seem to
        resist poking with a stick.

My Father Gave Us a Wendy-Bird

> Then all went on their knees, and holding out
> their arms cried, "O Wendy lady, be our mother."
> J. M. Barrie, *Peter Pan and Wendy*

Finally, my father brought
us a Wendy-bird. We shot her out of the sky
    with our bows and arrows. She woke up

        and made us turkey and stuffing—
it was the first day of summer. My father
    took group pictures with the timer

        and the flash, running
to get in the frame. My dead
    mother hovered somewhere

        near in that moment. My brothers
and I fought bitterly for attention,
    an old reflex. We were fighting

        so hard to impress the Wendy,
I was afraid someone would accidentally knock
    Lucy off the balcony. Windbags,

all of us, our achievements, our
years on the storm-tossed sea of
    orphanhood. Wendy-bird struggled

    to keep up. My father looked on adoringly.
Douglas was mean. He said he just
    got back from the Far East — why were we

    talking about Carrollton, Georgia? Tinkerbell,
God bless her, knocked over Douglas's
    Drambuie, soaked the tablecloth.

    I expected worse. I saw all of Wendy's peculiar
antiques going down. I couldn't decide
    about her things. Were they

    tacky, overly ornate (the music cabinet,
nymphs painted on top, etc.) — what would Mother
    say? Despite her preternaturally

    blond pixie, impossibly
smooth skin, the Wendy-lady was real
    enough, with her special boot

    for recent bunion surgery. She was
wholesome, she played
    the piano. My father

    stood behind her, his hands
on her shoulders
    in the photo.

October

       Why the sudden attraction to
Eggs? O centerless one,
     O selfless one. The

       Big plump runny center,
Sunflower yellow, source of power
     And joy. Compacted

       Energy as a seed's. I am
Drawn there. Over-easies three times a week.
     (Early, so that I have

       Something to go on.)
I never ate eggs! And the birds on the wire,
     What's that about, O

       Centerless one, trying
To catch a scrap of what
     They're saying. Birds upon

       Birds lined up uniformly, or flying
Like an errant scarf turning
     Itself inside and out, ace fighter pilots

Performing aerostunts. Squish squish,
I'm in the yolk, the center
Of all understanding. Katherine

Is in there with me,
But that's another story. And from
In there, the overflowing

Viscous, juicy self, I understand
French, on my French immersion
CD with real-life vignettes about

Fishing, sporting events, and
Christmas shopping, and yes,
The language of birds: travel

Routes, who gets to
Sit where . . . . Down by the levee the starlings
Congregate. Everyone

Scurrying, to Borders, to
Juniper, the new clothes shop, to the movies —
I'm looking up at

The long, long wire. Morse
Code of birds' bodies. Fat body, the dot —
Bare wire, dash.

Terminal

Airport as lung. My mother's
carcinomic lung. Little men in uniforms running
around it, checking. Big men

with Uzis. Filipino's
backpack as lung. The uniforms keep sending it
back through while the sullen

young man flips through *Surfer* magazine.
I see it on the x-ray screen, lung of yellow
and red and green clusters — is

it metastasizing? I'm checked at countless
formica-topped tables. I'm afraid this is an innard
I'll never get out of, the terminal

where I keep producing my ID and they
keep referring me to another person
with a wand. Wand up, wand down,

wand between my legs. And what is in
my make-up kit, my sandals? I am a suspect
in the system. I have

a little invisible red flag somewhere
by my name because I bought a one-way ticket. A one-
    way ticket? I won't

    be released. This is a white
institution; I'll be ushered up and down an escalator
    into a deeper room,

    a cabin where they'll issue
me an oxygen mask, like the one my mother had. Large
    and clear, clamped on my face.

    First, they ask for my keys, my wedding
ring, my watch. Then my glasses.
    Then, the clothes I wore here. Is this an airport?

    Uniformed, they put me on a rolling
bed. People with names like Tammy
    come in and out, officiously, and without

    warning, introduction. They just show up
and prod. It's blood pressure, vitals, and catheter
    bag; it's morphine pump,

    then morphine drip. They show up
every 20 minutes, as I dip further and further from
    their world, without fail, to bathe,

    to turn, to check. They lift my thin
hospital gown. They wipe me down; they run a tiny
    sponge around my lips.

Always someone different, a shift
change. When will I get out of this
　　lung that will not stop

　　　　dividing? From the rear of the
cabin, I see a freckle-faced man in a dark suit,
　　with a clipboard, heading toward

　　　　me. I try to get up. A pilot
materializes, wearing a stethoscope, a navy blue
　　cap. Sit down, he says,

　　　　I knew you before you knew
yourself. I know your downsitting and your
　　uprising — his sweating face

　　　　so close to mine I can almost
smell his TicTac. Relax, he says, Time is
　　daylight savings, temperature

　　　　above normal, wind
from the southeast, no precipitation likely,
　　in the city where you're going.

On Mount Saint Francis
Over Goldengrove Unleaving

        The finch perches insouciantly on St. Francis's
head and lets fly its song. Márgarét, áre you léaving?
        It's like we're on our cell phones

                again, saying, "I can't hear you, you're cutting
out." Blanks at the critical moments, what
        exactly was so compelling

        about that Swedish author whose
book you edited, whom you never met? This critical
        moment I'm here at Mt. Saint

                Francis deluding myself about being
an author and you, dear Margaret, are, as they say,
        under the knife. The last time I saw you

                you wore leopard-spotted silk gloves,
and threatened to step on my daughter's new white
        shoe. Who wouldn't be furious?

        I sit beside a sign which bears
these words: "As the deer / longs
        for / running water, / so my soul / longs for you /

my God," along with a primitive
painting of a monk staring into extremely
turbulent white water, nothing like the tame

pool beneath, the size of a bathtub
into which what appears to be an
upturned hose spurts water.

About the size of the
pool and fountain you had dug outside
your bedroom before going to

the hospital. You planned to open
the window and hear
it from your bed during your convalescence.

Márgarét, are you léaving? I kept evoking
that poem, on those Saturday phone dates, knowing
you probably couldn't hear

me through the obscured connection.
Are you grieving? Those surgeons are relieving
you of a rather critical body part and

replacing it with a makeshift
arrangement. No matter! Did I tell you what it was like
visiting John at the Milner

Nursing Home? He was shrunken
and in pain but fierce and aware as ever. As I
am approaching 50, which you remind me

you're not yet,
I have a different view of old people.
　　　After all, my own face startles me in the

　　　mirror. My own Jackself,
staring back at me, unveiled by youth or cuteness. Anyhow,
　　　I see them now as perfectly

　　　fresh selves, in unfresh bodies. Not original,
I know. But it took me a while
　　　to know why I weep.

Psychoanalytic Vacation

Featuring my deceased mother as stone,
or stone as mother. Cool brown stone. Polished
    stone that she kept on the bedside

        table, stone she loved to hold. Two years
later it is still there. On a white plastic oblong tray
    with pink birds painted on it. My father

        as tenor in the barbershop
quartet. Fifth act in the Westminster-Canterbury retirement
    home Spring Follies. On the grainy

        videotape, he is stooped, his glasses
large; he is hard to distinguish from the other
    palsied oldsters. I hope what I'm hearing

        is not the falsetto he said the ringleader
forced him to sing. Ellen, his lady friend,
    is the accompanist, attendant

        fairy. We watch the video in her
apartment. Each room a tiny replica
    of one at her country homestead. The furniture

crammed in. I sit on a maroon-patterned
hard-stuffed Prince Somebody chair with footstool.
        Ellen is resting her hair

        and wearing a turban. A voluminous
caftan on her tiny body. I imagine she is glad
        to see me. That she leaves

        a mint for me on the fresh, white
pillow in her replica guestroom. At our meal
        of leftovers in Ellen's tiny dining room,

        I stare into the shiny oval
surface of her heirloom mahogany table. I remember
        coming home from Salt Lake

        fourteen years ago, tired.
I am sure Mother was tired. I'd worked so hard.
        I had a baby! I'd passed

        my grad classes, had succeeded at, or
at least not fucked up, my teaching. I had
        it in my mind, that after

        my long absence, my hard work,
in my white linen A-line skirt that she had given me
        the summer before, that was so

        respectable, she would be at the airport
to greet me. In fact, she didn't feel up to it.
        Or she had never intended

to come. I was delivered
by my father, with husband and baby,
to the guest house. I can't remember

now whether she was up
when we came in. Ellen asks me over the abysmal
dinner of to-go containers

from the cafeteria (I think: So much
ocean around, yet I can't get a decent piece
of fish out of these people to

save my life!) about my thirteen-year-old
daughter, then segues to my own
adolescence. How was it? I am

Narcissus yanked into the shiny
surface of her oval table. I couldn't
find my reflection until I was

in my forties, I say, and she tries
desperately to backpedal, to soft pedal, while
my bitterness foments. My father

looks stunned, or willfully
vacant. How do they keep the old people from
jumping out of the window,

I suddenly ask myself. Then I remember
earlier that day, trying to peer out my dad's 11th floor
window, I learned that it opened only

six inches! You'd have to do it
off the living room balcony, at a cocktail party, in full
view of everyone, and that

wouldn't be polite! But, there is
no mint, no pillow waiting for me on a freshly made-up
Murphy bed at Ellen's. I am to sleep

upstairs in my dad's apartment, next to
my mother's stone. Those summers, she left me
a vase of just-opened gardenias, which

filled the guest house with their
ambrosial scent. Crusty Italian bread, orange juice,
cereal, bananas — and bacon

in the freezer. A letter from an
old family friend she thought I might like to read. Or
a clipping. Like the overly

kissed forehead of the statue
of some saint, I wonder if the stone bears the
imprint of her hand. I put it on

my chest, ignoring the sound of the
hallway door opening and my father's retreating
footsteps to the cement fire escape

and down to Ellen's
apartment. Mother, I touch your solitude
and grief. Now I can sleep.

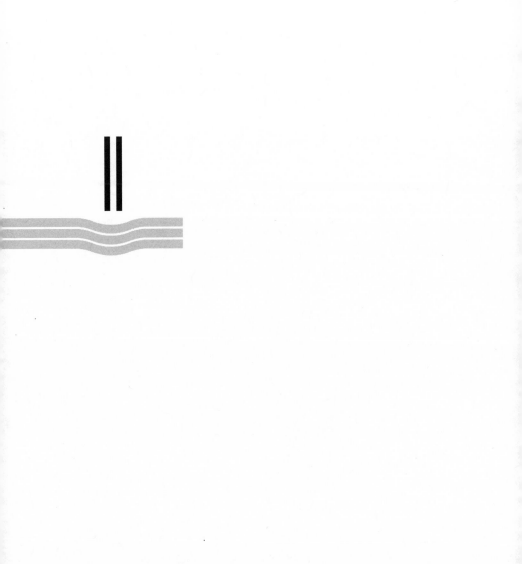

Midwestern Summer
My Dead Mother as Muse

My mother doesn't
like me nosing into her life
in the afterlife

any more than she
liked me nosing into it
in this one. Witness, the

ratcheting buzz of the cicada —
that's her way of saying,
Bug off.

Josie gets to do it. Her mother
loved her. She made a little shrine
with a skull knife

on it and her mother
knocks the knife down, says hello. My mother
teases me with thistle fluff,

wafting by my windshield
as I sit stalled in traffic on I-94
in Chicago. I am dying

to go to the bathroom, creep
inch by inch for two hours. Thistledown,
nonchalant fairy, drifts unharmed

between the twin axles
of a Mack truck. On the prairie,
my mother lures me into watching

the beautiful dragonfly,
brown bars embossed on its
glistening transparent wings,

its little white lobster
tail curled under; she lets me think it
a shining emissary from the

other world, then laughs
when I open the folklore
reference book and discover

that the dragonfly, often known
as the "mosquito hawk,"
is also nicknamed "the Devil's

darning needle" and likes to
sew children's mouths shut — their noses, ears,
and whole heads, too, if

necessary — when they speak
out of turn. Likewise, the bronze diamond-patterned
snake reclining in the path —

she lets me mull that one
over, as I leap three feet in the air.
        The orange monarch with black

        and white spotted regal
head resembles her. It lands on a sprig
        of golden rod, looks at me

        priggishly, asks me to pay
obeisance. The petals of each lavender cone flower
        chirp *love me, love me not* through the

        whole damned meadow. I never end up
with the petal I want. Goldfinches follow their
        zigzag radar, while I lurch off

        in search of the new ripe
blackberries my mother leaves for me
        every day on the bush

        under the horse chestnut.
Then suddenly a bramble pops
        up from the path

        and hooks my leg:
"Do you think it's a picnic
        here in the Bardo?"

        Purple lupine, black-eyed Susans.
The shining hip-high grass. Coming around
        a curve in the newly

mown path, I flush a flock
of wood thrushes. Among them is a blue bird—
gorgeous, preternatural.

I remember the new
black silk pantsuit I wore at my mother's
funeral, as if I could ever

approach the dead's
iridescent splendor. I hear the sound of
birdcall, my mother's

laughter, watch the exotic
bluebird vanish down the creek bed
into the thicket of

the other world,
leaving me to choke
on the dust of this.

Mud Cap

Father Dan says the shepherds
who went to see the baby Jesus were
dirty. Dirty! I never

saw that in a whole
lifetime of eyeing crèches. Big
ones in churches, tiny ones

on mantlepieces, poster board
2-D cutouts in the flatbed
of a parked pickup,

lit-up, downtown, next to the
courthouse. They'd always looked
crisp as though

they'd just had showers — nor
was there any poop
in the straw — that goes

without saying. Mary was of
course immaculate, Joseph pressed,
and so on. The sheep's woolly white coats

were not stained. Father Dan's
proclamation, and he is always
     talking about reversals

          in the story of Jesus,
brought to mind the muddy
     portobello cap I found in

          Marsh Supermarket and bought to
take into my class, hoping someone would
     choose it from among the odd

          vegetables and fruits — radicchio,
red onion, Belgian endive, chicory, lemon, papaya,
     turnip or sweet potato — to

          write about. It was so dirty
there was really no
     hope of it ever getting

          clean, like those
sexy mechanics, who replace your u-joint and
     you think, so sexy and so dirty,

          what woman lets him get in
bed with, put his hands on, her?
     I loved the stubbornness

          of the moon-surfaced, pocked,
cratered mushroom cap. Because I was
     about to lose my job. Someone

cleaner, some*ones* cleaner
and less problematic were being brought in
        to interview, and, man, by comparison

        to my "performance," it was
obvious either one of them
        would function like a well-oiled

        machine. Making work disappear
rather than making work. Who can blame
        my colleagues for wanting them? For panting

        slightly, lips parted, when
anticipating their visits, as if watching
        an ice-dancing or gymnastics competition?

        Jesus did not compete, Father Dan
said it today. He said his addresses to the
        Pharisees, and so on, were not like

        our current president's "thank you"s
to the voters and fundraisers at the State
        of the Union address. Yet, I like my job,

        like bringing in homely vegetables
for my students to write about,
        even if no one chooses the bad-ass

        stubborn mushroom
and they turn instead to the firm
        carambola, starfruit;

they grab my sharp
knife and cut the ribbed dirigible crosswise
into perfect star-shaped slices,

offer them around, well-oiled
little vehicles of wonder, of night,
of royal beauty bright.

He Read the New Yorker Aloud to Me and Spoonfed Me Pieces of Cantaloupe
Le Coup de Foudre

They were on the lake.
Giant conductor

of electricity
     in an electrical storm

     metal canoe.
Back at the marina

     things started flying
objects wouldn't

stay in their places.
     Dan's license was in

the car Don took to
     go and see if the canoe

     had made
landfall somewhere else on the lake.

Don's camera — or what
     we presumed to be Don's camera —

showed up in Claire's bag
        so I took it.

           Claire and I both looked at the
           "Minolta" like what the fuck

      is this. All the cell phones
were with the wrong

                    people containing the
          wrong numbers

plus there was no
        reception at

         the wharf. Claire
was weeping and

crumpled when we saw
        a streak of lightning

touch the lake.
               We were talking about 9-1-1

      and how to reach it — where was
the land line — were

             groping the little boat rental shack
         and tackle shop

and the obsidian-faced proprietor
        told us to calm down.

He wouldn't take a boat, another
          metal boat (he didn't say), out to look.

    But quietly after a few
minutes, after my asking naively

          several times about the Coast Guard
he silently threw a poncho

over his head
          and went out to

    a dinghy with an outboard
tied at the first slip in

          the dock. Don offered to go with him
but then decided to take

          the land route. Claire melted down
and I couldn't stand it.

When I got back to the house,
          Eleanor had gone on to

    Claire's with Jin and
    Patti, Claire's son and daughter,

          Erin, Patti's friend, and Claire. After
bringing Lucy and me

to the house, Dan went back
to work. (Bizarrely, he'd been

on his lunch hour.)
                    Lucy and I waited

        for Don whom we visualized bombing/
                    bouncing across Between the Lakes

Road to Isola Bella.
        Isola Bella (island with the school for the deaf) was where

                    the marina guy had
            found them — huddling in-

                    land and Dan near the
canoe. And then, later, from Claire's, Eleanor

        called and asked for an
e-mail address from

                    her purse and that's
                    when Don found

her fake ID
            moving her birthday up

                    well past the age necessary
        for a tattoo (her later-stated

                    purpose for the ID), straight up
            to one year past the legal drinking

age. Conveniently enough
            for her week alone in

        DC two months ago —
        Eleanor was on the

cell phone lying like a
            banshee. Something about

                an age requirement for a
tattoo. Then at Claire's,

later, trying not to get
        into Eleanor's punishments,

            and Claire and I started
                talking about

Nicole and William and Sandy and
            Barbara Meck and Judy

        and Judy's hair filled
        with her and David's sweat

                and cum, what have you.
        I accidentally blurted

out to Claire I never
            made as much money

in the bar as you did
        I never had the guts to

take the drugs you took. She blushed
and put her finger to her

lips. Her son
was watching TV in the dark on the bed

in her and Dan's bedroom off the kitchen
with Eleanor, and Patti

and Lucy were watching
Friends reruns in the

living room adjacent.
I told about Judy

her hair sopping
with David's juices

her asking me to help
comb the unruly mess

when she got to the bar
and my agreeing — not

telling her David had been
my lover before her and before

John Hall's ex whose name
I've forgotten (the one who'd

been on tour with a play,
who sent a shoe and a note

saying "The other shoe has dropped")—
and the Thanksgiving I picked

        her up for some restaurant
    dinner/event in the country.

      She plopped in my front seat, disheveled,
        said, "My pelvis is mush."

Judy, day waitress, was a chemist,
    as unlikely I said to Claire

      as Darlene being a psychic.
       Catherine killing herself

on 250 coming into town
      in the falling snow after a late night

    at the Greenbrier out there
    in the foothills.

       Darlene said at the séance
it was intentional.

      Frank saying goodbye to
us all

      shooting himself in a parked
    car at the end of Market Street,

wearing pantyhose, Todd told me.
    Claire said Frank had gathered

her and Molly together to say
goodbye, and I told

      her about his goodbye to me
    before I went to Atlanta, us

          standing on the threshold of the wooden
door we used

      for beer deliveries, Frank
smiling, drenched in the afternoon light.

      And how I ended up not going on
          to New Orleans (felt too unstable),

        then coming back up and being
told in Vinegar Hill, where

      I'd gone to the movies — maybe
David had told me.

      Then how the young waiter
    Paul Carleton had got me

        through the funeral. Not how we stood
   holding each other

      in a fountain on the downtown
mall after leaving Frank's parents' house. I said

I knew Frank well, we all did,
    he lived in the restaurant bathroom

after all.
And Claire told me

    something I didn't
    want to hear, something I hadn't

known, or hadn't remembered,
    how Frank had dressed

        as her, C & O waitress, at Halloween, replete
with pantyhose. I said I knew

    that he'd been a prostitute
in San Francisco but I hadn't

    thought too hard about what that
        meant. I said was he a transvestite,

    a transsexual, she said she didn't
    know but that dying in drag

    was surely a statement. I told her
about David's friend — was it Sam? —

killing himself on 20 North going into
or coming out of town

        hitting a tree, while loaded, maybe
not intentionally. How David was a mess,

    how I was trapped up there in that
apartment, the isle of Calypso, listening

to the same Rachmaninoff
piece over and over, smoking pot,

drinking Benedictine, or Cointreau, being fed cantaloupe
by the spoonful, and having endless

frantic sex while David wept
and baked something — scones? — that Sam had liked,

to take to the wake.
I didn't talk about the dress I wore, since my

husband was standing there, in Claire's kitchen,
that I wore for days, the summer

air, fragrance of a magnolia tree streaming
in the flung-open French windows, gardenias,

the omnipresent fan,
the sounds

of Roger, David's major professor, and his family
in the apartment below, the dress

with brown and gold flowers — whose had it
been originally? — that opened in the

front. How David and I had gotten
together, not the details about the "double

date" with Nicole where she'd slept
with David, and me with C., waking up

at her country house, "Hollywood,"
and catching a glimpse of Nicole's

  perfect bare ass through a door, as she
    sprawled face down on

      a white-sheeted bed.
  A brunch not long after, where C. was

    with Rebecca, his longtime girlfriend, of whom
I'd known nothing, and I was being

        "transferred"/pimped out to David (Nicole
      was through with him)—I figured it

out as we were driving away, to my
    place out in Farmington, me at the wheel,

      David reading to me from the *New Yorker*.
(A professional lover he was.)

    I told her I'd seen David years later
      and he intimated his alcohol and drug

        abuse was kind of stalling him there,
      he hadn't made any more movies

or finished his doctorate—he had
    the job I'd had, as the

day bartender. How we'd lived on veal sweetbreads,
    the hangover cure, those Dijon vinaigrette-

soaked Boston lettuce salads, real butter
pressed into white bone ramekins, Sarah's

homemade peasant bread, and filet
mignon. I told Claire

about David's obsession with his Latin wife
who'd abandoned him for some

politician in Venezuela, writing
him long letters begging to come back—

the threat of Madia's return was very
much in the air that Thanksgiving day when

I picked up Judy. (As it happened, she
fucked the daylights

out of David right up to the hour,
practically, that Madia resurfaced.)

I was having a
breakdown, withdrawing

from one thing, taking up
another, and knew

to be grateful that I'd never
been in love with David

though I'd certainly had a hard
time living without him when he vanished.

My daughters were in
the boat that had not

come in. My two children,
with Claire's husband and son;

my husband was
running around on the dock, soaked.

Looking out on the lake
trying to make out their boat.

It was raining so hard
there was no visibility.

It was chilling to see
Eleanor's photo there like

a mug shot — an organ
donor, on the fake

driver's license
with the seal of Florida

embossed all over it
in mother-of-pearl iridescent ink.

After we found it, I told her I'd call
the police if I caught her

breaking the law again.
        Eleanor said could you not

           use those horse
        analogies with me, those dog,

           the "rein," the "leash" —
as in "tighter rein," "shorter leash."

        And Judy, unlikely
chemist from Pennsylvania

      somewhere,
          science nerd,

      turned to me from the passenger
            seat in the old beige

        dinged volkswagen, "Arthur,"
that honked pitifully

at every right turn, Judy, whose dank
           and mossy, love-drenched

          hair I'd had my hands in
      from the first time

I met her, who I'm sure David
     called "Pobrecita," as he

had me, looking ravaged in the November
     chill, at 10 A.M.,

said, "I don't think
I'll ever walk again. The whole

bottom
            half of my

            body is pulverized. My
pelvis is mush."

I Need Scarf Lessons

Crack the Whip is a simple outdoor children's game
[which] is usually played in small groups, either on grass
or ice. One player, chosen as the "head" of the whip, runs
(or skates) around in random directions, with subsequent
players holding on to the hand of the previous player. The
entire "tail" of the whip moves in those directions, but
with much more force toward the end of the tail.
Wikipedia

It was crack the whip all winter,
in a basement room, Sunday morning
meditation meeting, chairs

in a disheveled coil. Crum Creek,
forty years ago, in Swarthmore,
Pennsylvania, frozen

over, brittle tree limbs
scratching the leaden sky. Rough boys
I didn't recognize

playing pick-up hockey
or gathering us in a sloppy
labyrinthine spiral, holding

hands, so the outside person
could take off like a rocket, whipping
us back and forth until

the kids in the tail
broke off. Trying not to think of my
sixteen-year-old

daughter in a foreign
country, in trouble. Reports she was ill, in
despair, and on the verge of

being thrown out of, if not
the country, the district, where
she'd been placed. Finally, a few

weeks later, in the cusp
between seasons, I left that room,
visited her in her new

home, in the suburbs of Paris,
and found her so radiant I was afraid
she was pregnant. Thank God

it turned out not. She'd
flown off that whip and landed with a kind
family, in a tiny apartment, on

rue Louis Braille, her scarf
in a fetching coil, then loop, then tail.
She walked ahead of us in the city

always, because she knew
the way. She didn't look back as she
    led us from Le Gare du Nord to

      the metro, from La Place de la Concorde
to L'Orangerie. Once she led Lucy and me
    along the outside of an iron

      knee-high curb railing on a
busy street to a crosswalk, only Lucy and I
    did not know we were in

      a bus lane until the leviathan
bore down on us, honking. Eleanor already
    up on the curb, poised to cross, me

      cursing her in the wind, an
uncomprehending fierce-looking woman in a bun
    near us, looking at

      my mouth snarl
and make grotesque shapes, I suppose.
    I need scarf lessons, today's lacy

      white one hanging like a
hank of overcooked vermicelli
    around my neck, as I cross

      the courtyard to Starbucks
from my office, breathing the fresh
    silken air of spring, slammed

by wind, ignoring
the tornado threat around the edges. I imagine
my beautiful daughter up

ahead, wending her way
across the flagstones, her father, sister, and I
clinging for life at the tail, struggling

not to be flung off.

The Flossie Stories

I wasn't wrong to think
of her as drowning. Trying
to pull me under. I watched

my mother flail for 48
years. Then she went down. I came
up. Is this always the story

of mother and daughter? Talking
to my widowed father,
I realized she was mother to

her mother. And Flossie, my
grandmother, was always sinking. She'd had a
stroke. She lived in our

den on Cokes and Lucky
Strikes. She wheedled paregoric
from my father. He went

to the pharmacy,
said he needed it for his
children. The Flossie

stories, a controlled substance
when I was a child, are now loose
and proliferating,

ecstatic butterflies
unfurling from the fist of my mother's
agony. For example, the cats Flossie

thought she heard screaming
in the sofa springs — her nocturnal calls to
Dickie, then Dickie's to my newly married

mother in Philadelphia, followed
by yet another commitment
to Eastern State.

This winter, after my mother's
death, was sad. In my little Midwestern town,
red-haired Tommy Roy

showed up from Canada,
grinning in the newspaper, driving a
Zamboni. He was

there to start the town skating
rink. He hugged me twice, and I was ready to
run away with him. Little

wiry man with the booming
Canadian voice, he had great
stories to tell in 12-step meetings —

and the waxed handlebar
mustache. (Was that it? Was he like
my dapper grandfather in the

portrait, in his pink
hunting jacket?) A former hockey star and
coach, he traveled from

town to town making the
mirrored oval, with the piped-in music, where
the people of the town

could skate round and round
under the winter trees, trying to avoid wiping
out on the grooves made

by others' skates. I heard later
that the young girl who was hanging
around Tommy Roy

at the rink, whom I gathered
he'd met in one of our meetings, was his new
sweetheart. I was in love

with a two-timer! A guy who
chose someone barely out of high school,
who wore those absurd pastel comb-clips

in her short unruly hair. The plump,
blushing cheeks of a child. He worked near the river,
among the dark winter trees.

The dark winter place
where my mother
  fell in the ice, or did I only

  dream it? Fecund place
of memory. Crum Creek in Swarthmore. My
  mother was beautiful

  on her white skates,
mysterious in her grief. The water beneath
  the ice was muddy, milky.

  I kept dreaming she fell in.

Autumn Is Cusp

a stand of dead cone
flowers side by side with a choir

of deep-throated purple
penstemon, tiny mouths

open, beard tongues wailing silently.
Ebullient red

and orange celosia flaming
at their base, meadow rue

hovering. Red hollyhocks, black-eyed Susans,
pink primroses, morning glories.

A cloud
of small gnats staying with us

following us. Sticking
to Sally's snout. Her white face,

my light blue t-shirt specked. Is it the mind
that draws us forward?

The car that climbs up, as in Saturday's dream — my car —
    a vault, as if predestined,

        instructed, but somehow leaving the
            other cars, headlights on

in the coming dusk, winding
            patiently below. The winding road

        around the Wissahickon, Conshohocken.
Falling dark. The nursing home in

            Pennsylvania where
    my aunt Clara lived her last days,

            her husband Robert, senile, in
the basement, Stapley Hall.

            Not far from the slum
where my father grew up. Or Rock

        Creek Parkway that I went
            running above last year this time

            in DC, in Rose Park,
where the prosperous Georgetown mothers

            strolled their attractive
babies. The cars curving orderly

        below. Patient, aligned, piled up at stoplights
in compact rows, like dishes.

And me, above, going where? As if
        in Union Station, or Paddington,

           up near some curved invisible
           arch. Climbing. Where is

           everybody? And what is holding
me up? If I put in the clutch, if

           I turn off the key, will
        the car know then that

           the air is not a salty bouncy ocean
        and plummet down?

I dare not stop. Who is with me?
        Is anyone up there with me

in the ceiling? The night sky. Car.
Cusp. In West Lafayette

           traffic, in my waking life, why
        does it surge and try

to bolt like the nags from riding
        lessons in fourth grade, who

walked around the ring nearly dead till a whiff
           of the barn made them

           possessed. Car with its own mind.
Bucking, levitating,

                    bouncing. Last night,
I got in it after my awful

          day and the thing would not
obey the road. Nor my

                    hands posed reflexively
on the wheel. What was

          it that she said? That they were planning
                    to interview people

for my job? I imagined a note today
          when Sally and I

          set out, "It was just
too ugly." Then, later, better, after walking up

the creekbed road
in the park improbably named Happy Hollow. Compared to

the suffering
          I have read about

in the last 24 hours, the hunted
          and tortured, compared to our sponsored

                    daughter Sugey's puffy face in the
Children International photo. No longer hiding

          what it is like
to live in poverty,

in deprivation, Barranquilla . . . . Winding up
is like winding

down. This summer back and forth
                across the Appalachian spiny

mountains, as if actually making a journey. East,
Midwest. Midwest, East.

                With my books my papers.
        You can't tell sometimes

             in those switchbacks whether
up or down. Must be the grade. Steep cliff

cut away on either side. Sometimes, valley vistas, or
             a tunnel through rock. In my ascent

             in the dream
        oh it was certainly up. So up I was

dizzy. And the car wanted to fly last night, on
           the interstate,

             when I left work after the
        double-crossing day. Fly. Aunt Clara took

        me to the Wissahickon. Did we walk?
             She rescued me from my suburban home,

where my mother was possessed. I
took the train to

30th St. and changed to get to
Germantown. The streets were brick. There was the bit with

the garbage and the chute
in the wall by the elevator

on her floor, where we got to
drop unwanted coffee grounds

and broken egg shells down
four floors to the incinerator.

She saved me. That was
before Jessica Savitch, Philadelphia

newswoman, left Odette's in New Hope one night
with her lover, drove straight into the creek

and drowned. Was it the Wissahickon?
The time I visited Clara

and had dinner in the dining
room at Stapley Hall, her stubborn pin curl

plastered to her cheek,
her sup-hose knee socks, bare trees

on three sides of the dining room in the fading light. Like
witnesses, like emaciated humans. Like scrawny legs.

The weird sense
that in the dead of winter

they were growing. We circled our choices
    with stubby pencils — prunes or

tomato juice — on the mimeographed sheets.
Certainly years before Salt Lake City

        and the October snows
that started at sundown with the horizontal sideswiping wind and tiny

        ping-pong balls whipped along, lashing.
            The temperature would drop 50 degrees

        in an hour. When I was a child,
deep in the Swarthmore woods a woman left a note

        in one of her loafers
    and laid her head down on the trestle

in the path of an oncoming
        train. Did my mother

have "Seasonal Affective Disorder"? Honey,
I think it would be safe

        to say so. Or maybe just "This is mean," referring
            to the situation at my job,

        my marriage. Or maybe just life in general.
Autumn is cusp. Is car. Is Keats.

The car tried to step
before an approaching furniture truck

white with blue trim. I shut my eyes. I
told it no.

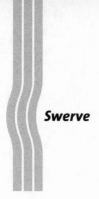

Swerve

        I dreamt I was in a car
floating, in horizontal free-fall
      on the ice

        on Harrison Bridge,
then steering like crazy
      or methodically

        not into the skid, I think
now, as taught, but against it
      but still cool-headed—

        quick— the cars
around me hanging back while
      I catapulted from lane to lane

        and up on a
raised triangular island separating the merging
      lane, like it was

        nothing, the bollixing blunderbuss
Volvo, its enormous ass
      and chassis.

Eventually coming out, crawling
home on a sheet of ice
        shaking, unable to tell

        if the axle was bent, the
road still gliding under me. Only it wasn't
        a dream, so I do wish I had

        remembered the skid rule—
on ice one doesn't have that feeling
        of mastery as in snow; it's

        bald terror. At work that
morning, I took a full and boiling cup from
        the microwave with my

        left hand because
the right was full. And then
        sloshed boiling water

        on my hand and cried
out in an un-office-like way
        like a bull or a woman

        in childbirth. Bellowed.
And Mason called out from
        his office, his door was

        open, Mason who'd had
the sweet stray dog the other day
        on a bit of rope, on one

of the days it was snowing
and nearly zero, Are you all right?
And I said, I shouldn't

have taken the cup out
with my left hand. And he said
I thought you'd burned

yourself. I said
I should have known I could not
trust my left hand

and he said, Do you
have tendonitis? And I said, Something
like that, I just can't

trust . . . . This
to the person who voted to have me fired
two weeks before, letting

him off the hook
as I had the day with the stray. And Reid,
whenever I caught a glimpse

of him, simply looked red
as a steak, as a piece of
rare meat, and I couldn't

gather the connection — had
he suddenly developed high blood
pressure? Slim, young, fresh-faced

athletic Reid? Who graciously
squired me to lunch and dinner
		on the day of my presentation? All

		from casting a simple vote of
betrayal? I flatter myself! Dramatize.
		Drawing a hot bath, after

		unloading the car, hauling
my day's books and papers over glazed
		snow clumps, lecturing myself

		not to dwell on the ice
incident any more than necessary,
		having left my sleeping

		husband a note for
the morning, about the possible bent
		chassis, the axle — getting into

		the scalding tub, I decided
God had looked after me, yes, but
		also maybe my mother,

		the genius of the
car, which she gave me five years ago
		when she knew she was dying,

		and who wasn't mad at me
after all, did not think of me as
		betraying her with those

poems, those statements
in public interviews,
   and was hovering around

      in white, or another pale color,
protecting me. . . . I am not being facetious
   here, or in any way mocking

      and sarcastic, when I say
yes for those buoyant three minutes
   six days ago when I saw

      Bill, I was able to manufacture
being in love. I got very high
   and started to float rudderless —

      it was helium to think
he might feel that way too
   but then I thought I was making it

      up, and later, much later,
with the help of that busybody
   Katherine, that I simply wanted

      an escape from the pain of my
marriage. Tedious. Excuse me. Hence the
   fantasies of gardening, bird-watching,

      hell, maybe even snowshoeing, laughing,
and receiving cunnilingus in
   a rushing river. I talked to myself about

death after the ice episode. What
was I so afraid of? A lot of noble, worthy-to-be-on-earth,
        worthier, had already

            been taken—why not me? But the
unbearable crushing grief of thinking
        of my daughters grieving made

            me glad again that it had
simply been a scary, swervy moment
        and perhaps a damaged wheel rim or bent

            axle. I won't bring up that outdoorsy
Bill again or that sword of Damocles
        my husband is dangling over

            my head, has been for three-plus
years—his suddenly ambidextrous
        sexual leanings—that keeps

            me from feeling I have a
shield, or whatever it is
        that married people

            feel about their spouses. Keeps me
from feeling cozy. Does anyone
        feel cozy? Ice is cozy they say

            after a certain amount
of exposure. Free fall, it was like,
        then the dead man's spiral. Sideways, the car

hulking, embarrassingly large,
like the time I had a sort
of elephantiasis anxiety attack.

I was four, felt I was growing huge,
quickly. I'd been
having my picture

taken in my new puffy-sleeved
red voile dress on the
bench in the front hall

with my brothers. Had
my mother made
a cutting remark? I was suddenly

enormous. No one would want
me then. Was that my bigger fear? I should
have known better than

to trust the left hand.

If You Step Off Now

Waking from her nest
of blankets, my rumpled
plump seatmate in

maroon sweatwear asks, "Is it time
to get off?" as though she
would step off

into cloud. I say, "If
you step off now
you'll be in heaven."

That's what Dad and
Ellen call it: I say,
"How's Sonny?" and

Dad says, "Oh, he
went to heaven." Apparently, in one
of my lapses — one Saturday

when I forget to
call — there has been yet
another funeral for someone

at Dad's retirement
place. Which they shrug off
        like a grocery

            shop, a step off
with carry-on bag into
        a neutral, disinterested

            cloud layer. The pilot over
the PA makes a point
        to tell us it's morning

            as if we could have
turned the world
        upside down,

            entirely, in our overnight flight,
and declared it sunset, the slant
        golden light strobing

            the cabin, our foreheads.
"Sharon" had to crawl on all fours
        to wedge her bulk

            into the seat. Still,
she stroked and massaged her
        almost equally hefty

            husband, talked in a
low voice to him, slept against him —
        was never cross — the whole

flight; she turned her awkward
body around once or twice, kneeing me
in the process, to talk with her

sister, her sister's husband,
her toddler nephew, lodged
in the seats behind. She was,

they all were, her sister
told me, traveling to Norway for the
first time in twenty-

plus years to see the
old people. Not off on an
individual getting-away-from-it-all

junket, as someone I won't
name might have been said to be.
I can't say why I like

to hang between cities
in airplanes, willfully eluding
gravity, my life whittled

down to a suitcase,
looking out my porthole window
at the foamy celestial surf. Or

to roam the white
airport, while my children wail and thrash
in their plasticine sleeves

in my wallet. I troll dispassionately
the duty-free shops for the essentials
of this world — cameras, perfume,

watches — stacked so pleasingly
in their glittering cases, or the souvenir
stands, where people

like Sharon and her family
earnestly shop, for tokens of the mud, and wind,
and flowers of Holland,

the netherland below
the nowhere where I stand: a palm-sized
windmill, a paper bag

of tulip bulbs, and,
for walking buried streets and gardens,
a miniature pair of brightly stenciled

wooden clogs.

In the Truth Room

When the priest says *"this is my body,"* it is at that instant
when, through the miracle of transubstantiation, the bread
and wine which we offer as the bloodless sacrifice to our Lord
truly become the Body, Blood, Soul and Divinity of Jesus....
Perpetual Adoration is when the priest takes a consecrated host,
such as the one described above, and places it in a monstrance.
... The monstrance is then placed in front of the tabernacle (an
ornate box which holds the monstrance and any consecrated
hosts) or on the altar of the church or chapel for adoration.
Complete Handbook for Perpetual Eucharistic Adoration

In the truth room, in
    Chapelle du Saint Sacrement

in l'Eglise
Saint-Pierre, in Moissac,

    one has no choice but
to talk to God. Sign says

      "Cette Chapelle, lieu de silence
et de recueillement,

ne se 'visite' pas. Vous
            n'y entrez que si vous

            voulez vraiment prier."
So, damn tootin', I prayed.

            Or tried. Only the prayer was
brittle—no gush of

            gratitude, no overflow
of *I am loved*. The opposite.

            Quite. I'm not sure
if the Blessed Sacrament

            was in there. Think it
was, think that standing chalice-

            type thing, with the golden rays
coming out of it, was it. Don't

            come in if you don't want
            to pray. Don't come

just to "visit." I remember once
            in Carrollton, Georgia,

in the middle of nowhere,
            in the middle of hayfields and

            soybeans, of mules and roosters, I sat in Our
Lady of Perpetual Help, babysitting

the Blessed Sacrament.
I'd signed up on a sheet

which read "Adoration
of the Blessed Sacrament." I'd signed

up for one hour. Crude Catholic
that I was, I tried

to adore it, to keep my
meditation holy.

Likewise, yesterday, my recueillement.
But it was so black.

I simply don't know where
I belong—

as usual. I think
I had a better idea in Carrollton,

Georgia. I was hamstrung; I was
landlocked; I was cul-de-sacked; shanghaied;

in short, trapped. It was humid and miserable (Thank
God the church was air-conditioned) and

my children were young,
my husband was depressive, to put

it extremely nicely,
and I couldn't get work.

A lot to pray about!
While keeping it clean.

I thought, proudly, I was
good at meditation—I could

handle that hour. Turns out someone
else came in—did she think

she was signed up, or what?
She sat several pews behind

me silently. What was
she thinking about? Could have been anything.

Life was not altogether happy,
lacked middle-class sense of

self-importance, in rural Georgia. I
liked that, liked resting

from all that "aspiring." People threw
whole fast food meals

out on the shoulders of
the two-lane roads. Dead

German shepherds sat oozing
on the center yellow line

for days. "Who am I?"
These people never asked it. I had no

trouble with the Joneses. They sat
up in a deer stand drinking beer

and waving rifles. They were not worrying
that their book had not been

published! But it worried me
for the kids. How would they

get that essential transmission? Get
out of bad grammar, junk cars, and

duct-taped broken windows? Moissac.
I must return to the black

box of mind I sat in yesterday. Oh,
God, it's been rough, here in the gorgeous

South of France, without my
children, whom I miss unbearably, or

my husband, whom I would prefer not to miss. Just
not being altogether sure about

latent Peter Pan proclivities that
after twenty years of marriage

have suddenly surfaced. And then
the dream last night. A student e-mailed me.

Michael. Said I had a brother who'd been
killed, along with someone else I already

knew had been murdered, a family friend, in
the distant past. I was in a dark

room with a hardwood floor—a pub?
With pinball machines in the corners? I asked

my brothers and they looked
down (I'm just not sure of their ages in the

dream). Then my mother. Who took me
into a windowless room. A truth

room, black like
the Chapelle du Saint Sacrament, but with

no illuminated yellow, red, and blue
abstract stained glass above the

altar. No altar. Certainly,
no Blessed Sacrament. She was alive,

which actually I took no note of
in the dream, younger, black-haired, down-

cast, but telling her truth unguardedly. Did that ever
happen in life?

Yes, I think, when
I was young, she confided in

me openly. I loved that closeness, and
her, unbearably (except when I hated

her for mocking and humiliating me). There had
been a child who died. "My baby,"

she muttered quietly, almost rocking
herself. How old was he? I asked.

Twelve and a half.
What? How was it that I did not

know him? He would have been between
my brothers, or between my brothers

and me. And what about
the funeral, the awful

aftermath? Where was I? A creepy
feeling washing over me, transposed

from my fifty-plus-year-old waking life:
    Was my memory blanking again? Going black?

I asked her his name. She said
"Eric." Eric, Eric. I had an auburn-haired

lover, or I-wished-he-were-my-lover, Eric. Basically,
I was riffling through my past,

like so many pages, trying to find
him, between the pages, between the lines. Eric?

My lost brother. What could it mean? And
the truth room. With my resuscitated

mother? Or the message
that had tipped me off

from Michael my student. Who, come to
think of it, is Irish. Who come to think

of it more than resembles the
scrumptious Eric, and is just

about the age he was then. Michael,
toward whom

I have complex feelings, as I do
all the students I love who are thirty years

younger. In his case, I want him to cut the
pretty boy lifeguard theme

and get a life. I want to save
him from the twenty years

of happy horseshit I put in on the dilettante
circuit. How arrogant am I?

And I fear I am getting closer to understanding
the dream. Thank you, Dr. Lindsay,

who said every character in a dream
is a part of oneself. The truth room, indeed,

in which sits my sorrowful mother. Will
I ever live on the planet

without the image of her downcast
black-haired head at the very center, in the

truth room of my consciousness? Irreparably
sad. Inconsolable.

My own kind of Blessed Sacrament,
which, God help me, I cannot help

but adore.

A Note on the Author

Dana Roeser grew up in the Philadelphia area and was educated at Tulane University, the University of Virginia, and the University of Utah. She has been the recipient of an NEA fellowship, the Great Lakes Colleges Association New Writers Award, and the Jenny McKean Moore Writer-in-Washington Fellowship. She won the 2004 Morse Poetry Prize for her first book, *Beautiful Motion*. Her poems have appeared in *The Iowa Review*, *Harvard Review*, *Antioch Review*, *Southern Review*, *Northwest Review*, *Shenandoah*, and elsewhere, as well as on *Poetry Daily*. She lives with her husband and two daughters in West Lafayette, Indiana.

A Note on the Prize

The Samuel French Morse Poetry Prize was established in 1983 by the Northeastern University Department of English in order to honor Professor Morse's distinguished career as teacher, scholar, and poet. The members of the prize committee are: Francis C. Blessington, Joseph deRoche, Victor Howes, David Kellogg, Ellen Noonan, Stuart Peterfreund, and Guy Rotella.